Fun Fan Facts:
The Unofficial NBA Edition

Oklahoma City Thunder

Everything Young Thunder Fans Should Know

By: Jake Liam

Dedication

For the fans who kept the lights on in Oklahoma City when the big names left. You knew something the rest of the world didn't.

THE NBA BY THE NUMBERS

MOST NBA CHAMPIONSHIPS*

CELTICS (18) †

LAKERS (17)

WARRIORS (7)

BULLS (6)

SPURS (5)

As of the 2024-25 Season. † One Trophy = 4 Championships.

NBA HISTORY SNAPSHOT

1946 — NBA Founded

1954 — Shot Clock Introduced

1979 — 3-Point Line Added

2023 — NBA Cup Introduced

BIG NUMBERS

$156 million
Stephen Curry's est. earnings in the 24-25 season

7'7"
Tallest player in NBA history (Gheorghe Mureşan & Manute Bol)

30 | 4 | 82

30 — Teams Competing in the NBA

4 — Playoff Rounds

82 — Games Per Season

OKLAHOMA CITY THUNDER
IN THE NBA

- FOUNDED: 1967 †
- NBA TITLES: 2
- CONFERENCE TITLES: 5*

68 Wins in One Season (2024–25)

*† Founding dates are complicated & may cause arguments at Thanksgiving. Ask someone born before color TV. All Titles reflect pre-relocation franchise history. * As of 2024-25 Season.*

NBA ALL-TIME MVP LEADERS

KAREEM ABDUL-JABBAR (6) ★ MICHAEL JORDAN (5) ★ BILL RUSSELL (5)

EASTERN CONFERENCE

Atlantic – **Celtics**
Atlantic – **Nets**
Atlantic – **Knicks**
Atlantic – **76ers**
Atlantic – **Raptors**
Central – **Bulls**
Central – **Cavaliers**
Central – **Pistons**
Central – **Pacers**
Central – **Bucks**
Southeast – **Hawks**
Southeast – **Hornets**
Southeast – **Heat**
Southeast – **Magic**
Southeast – **Wizards**

WESTERN CONFERENCE

Pacific – **Lakers**
Pacific – **Clippers**
Pacific – **Warriors**
Pacific – **Suns**
Pacific – **Kings**
Northwest – **Nuggets**
Northwest – **Timberwolves**
Northwest – **Thunder**
Northwest – **Trail Blazers**
Northwest – **Jazz**
Southwest – **Mavericks**
Southwest – **Rockets**
Southwest – **Spurs**
Southwest – **Pelicans**
Southwest – **Grizzlies**

Introduction

Welcome, fans! Whether you're new to cheering for the Oklahoma City Thunder or you've been bleeding the team colors your whole life, this book is packed with fun, exciting facts about your favorite team. Get ready to impress your friends and family with everything you know about the Thunder.

Quick Timeout

This book is packed with stats. Like, A LOT of stats. Every fact was checked, double-checked, and triple-checked. But here's the thing about basketball history: not everyone agrees on everything. Ask someone who watched games before color TV and someone who grew up with instant replay and you'll get two completely different answers. My dad, stepdad, uncle, and grandpa all argued about the same fact. Four people. Four answers. All of them think they're right. So if you spot something that doesn't match what you've heard, congratulations. You might be a bigger fan than the people who helped make this book. And honestly? That's pretty cool.

HOW IT WORKS

THE SEASON
82 Games. One Goal.

Each team plays 82 games.
Win enough to make the
Playoffs.
Every game counts!

PLAYOFFS
30 Teams. 16 Make It.

8 per conference make the playoffs.
Win=Advance | Lose=Go Home
Best record
gets home court!

PLAYOFF ROUNDS
Best of 7. Win 4 or Go Home.

4 rounds of pure pressure.
Every series is do-or-die!

OVERTIME?
5 More Minutes.

Keep playing until
someone pulls ahead.
No ties. Ever.

THE FINALS
One Series. One Champion.

Winner lifts the Trophy.
Legend status unlocked.

How the NBA Works

At first glance, basketball feels simple. Ten players. One ball. Two hoops. Go.

Then the NBA adds the layers.

An 82-game regular season. A draft where bad teams pick first. Playoffs that last two full months. Superstars who can change everything with one trade. Dynasties that rise, fall, and rise again.

And somehow, it all works.

The NBA is built on one big idea: every team gets a chance to reset, reload, and rise again. No relegation. No dropping down to a lower league. Just basketball, every night, from October through June.

It is a league designed for drama, stars, and comebacks. And once you understand the flow, it is impossible to stop watching.

The League Setup

The NBA has 30 teams, spread across the United States and Canada. Those teams are split into two conferences:

- Eastern Conference
- Western Conference

Each conference has three divisions, mostly based on geography. Divisions matter for scheduling, but not as much as they used to.

Every team plays 82 regular season games, usually from October through April. Home games. Road games. Back-to-back nights. Long road trips. The season is a marathon before the sprint even starts.

Win games, and you climb the standings. Lose too many, and the pressure builds fast.

How Games Are Played

An NBA game has four quarters, each lasting 12 minutes. That means 48 minutes of game time, plus timeouts, free throws, and the occasional coach argument that adds another 20 minutes nobody planned for.

Scoring is simple:

- A shot inside the three-point line is worth 2 points
- A shot beyond the arc is worth 3 points
- Free throws are worth 1 point

If the score is tied at the end of regulation, the game goes to overtime, which lasts 5 minutes. Still tied? Another overtime. Keep going until someone wins.

There is a shot clock too. Teams have 24 seconds to take a shot. No standing around. No holding the ball forever. Keep it moving.

The Regular Season Race

The regular season is long for a reason. It tests everything.

Depth. Health. Focus. Patience.

Teams play opponents from both conferences, but they face conference rivals more often. By the end of the season, each conference's top teams have earned their playoff spots the hard way.

The goal is simple: make the playoffs. But there is a twist.

The NBA Cup

In 2023, the NBA added something new to the middle of the season. Something with actual stakes. They called it the In-Season Tournament, now known as the NBA Cup.

It works like this: Every team plays a small group stage during November and December, with special court designs that look like nothing else in basketball. The best teams advance to a knockout round held in Las Vegas.

The winners split a prize pool. Players earn bonus money. And for the first time, a team could lift a trophy before the playoffs even started.

Some fans are still warming up to it. Some players love it. But the moment a team starts treating it seriously and a crowd shows up buzzing in December, it feels like something.

Which, honestly, sounds about right.

The Play-In Tournament

Instead of sending the top eight teams from each conference straight to the playoffs, the NBA added something new. The Play-In Tournament.

Here is how it works:

- Teams ranked 1 through 6 in each conference are safe
- Teams ranked 7 through 10 fight for the final two playoff spots

The 7 and 8 seeds have an advantage. Win once and you are in. Lose and you still get one more shot. The 9 and 10 seeds have to win twice in a row just to earn a first-round matchup.

It turns the end of the season into a sprint. Every game suddenly matters more. Fans love it. Coaches age rapidly.

The NBA Playoffs

Once the playoffs begin, everything tightens.

Sixteen teams enter. Eight from each conference. Every round is a best-of-seven games series. That means the first team to win four games moves on:

- First Round
- Conference Semifinals
- Conference Finals
- NBA Finals

Home-court advantage matters. Crowds get louder. Rotations get shorter. Superstars play heavier minutes. One bad quarter can flip a series. One great performance can define a career.

By the time the NBA Finals arrive in June, only two teams are left. One from the East. One from the West.

Four wins away from a championship. Four wins away from history.

The NBA Draft: Hope Begins Here

Here is where the NBA gets clever. Every summer, new players enter the league through the NBA Draft. Teams take turns selecting college players, international stars, and teenagers straight out of high school.

The teams that finished with the worst records get the best odds to pick early through the Draft Lottery. It is not guaranteed, but it gives struggling franchises a real shot at changing their future with one pick.

That means one bad season does not doom you forever. It might actually change everything. Some franchises are rebuilt by a single draft night moment.

Hope shows up wearing a new jersey.

No Relegation. All Pressure.

Unlike many global sports leagues, NBA teams never drop down to a lower league. They always stay in the NBA.

That does not mean there is no pressure.

Fans remember losing seasons. Owners make changes. Coaches get replaced. Players get traded. Every year is a test of direction, patience, and belief.

Stars, Systems, and Showtime

The NBA is famous for its stars. But stars do not win alone.

Teams need chemistry. Coaches need systems. Role players need to deliver on the biggest stages. One injury. One hot streak. One trade deadline deal. Any of it can flip a season.

That balance between individual brilliance and team basketball is what makes the league special.

Fast breaks. Buzzer-beaters. Game 7s. And moments that get replayed forever. That is the NBA.

Once you get the flow, it is pure electricity.

Oklahoma City Thunder Facts

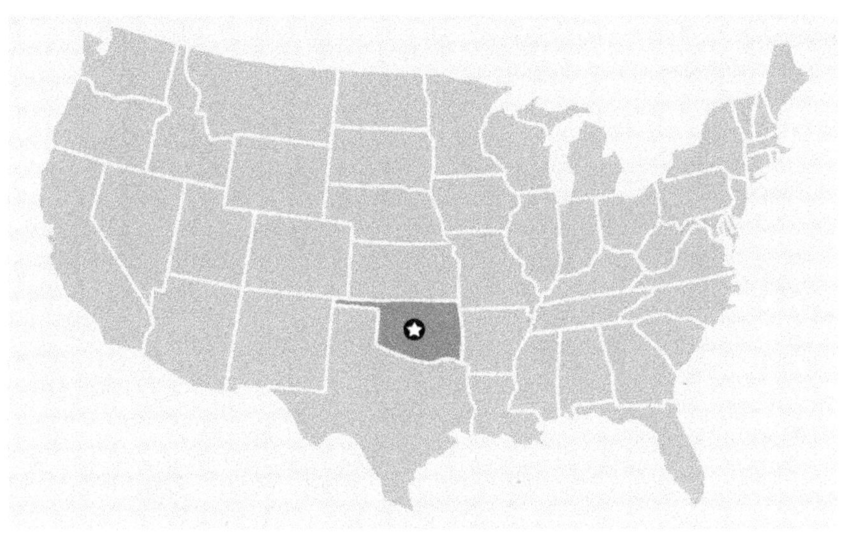

Home City

Oklahoma City, Oklahoma

Home City Metro Area Population

about 1.4 million

Home Arena

Paycom Center

Max Capacity: 18,203

Famous Local Food

Chicken-fried steak, onion burgers, BBQ, fried pies

Conference / Division

Western / Northwest

1. Born in Boeing Country

Seattle in 1967 was a city absolutely obsessed with airplanes. The Boeing Company had turned the entire region into an aerospace capital, and locals walked around with the kind of pride that only comes from knowing the most advanced flying machines on earth were being built in your backyard. So when Seattle landed an NBA expansion team and needed a name, the city did not exactly struggle with the brainstorming session. The SuperSonics. Named for supersonic jets. Fast, loud, and impossible to ignore. Other cities name their teams after bears or bulls or generic wildlife. Seattle named theirs after a jet that breaks the sound barrier. Respect.

The early teams were not quite as supersonic on the court. Being the first major professional sports franchise in the entire Pacific Northwest sounds glamorous until you realize it also means losing a lot of games in front of fans who are still figuring out how basketball works. Lenny Wilkens served as the team's player-coach, meaning he was simultaneously trying to run plays and run them himself, which is the sports equivalent of being your own boss and your own most difficult employee. Spencer Haywood arrived in 1971 as one of the most athletic forwards in the game and immediately gave Seattle something to actually get excited about. Fred Brown, nicknamed Downtown Freddie because he launched shots from distances that made his own coaches nervous, stuck around for fifteen seasons and became the heartbeat of the franchise.

Nobody was handing out championship trophies yet. But something real was being built in Seattle, one gloriously long jump shot at a time.

2. Seattle's Finest Hour: The 1979 Championship

Lenny Wilkens came back to Seattle in 1977, this time without a jersey, which was probably a relief for everyone. Just a clipboard, a coaching staff, and a team that had already made a surprise run to the 1978 NBA Finals before losing to the Washington Bullets in a way that left the city staring at the ceiling for weeks. Wilkens was not interested in a lengthy feelings discussion about that loss. He was interested in not repeating it.

The 1978-79 SuperSonics were legitimately fun to watch. Gus Williams was a blur at guard, the kind of player who could change the entire speed of a game just by deciding it was time to go. Jack Sikma anchored the middle with a shooting style so genuinely bizarre that it looked like he invented it in his driveway and nobody had the heart to tell him to stop. He would hold the ball high above his head before releasing it in a way that left bigger defenders completely baffled. It worked every single time, which is the most annoying possible outcome for everyone trying to stop it.

Seattle tore through the playoffs and rematched the Bullets in the Finals. This time the Sonics won, and downtown Seattle turned into the kind of celebration where strangers hug each other and nobody finds that weird. One championship banner went up in the rafters. For a franchise that had spent its first decade just trying to figure out what it was doing, that banner was everything. Seattle was a real basketball city now. It had the hardware to prove it, and Jack Sikma's inexplicable shot selection had contributed to every bit of it.

3. Gloves, Dunks, and the Night They Almost Beat the Bulls

Gary Payton talked. Constantly. To opponents, to referees, to the opposing bench, occasionally to the basketball itself. He was the point guard for the SuperSonics through most of the 1990s, and his defense was so suffocating that he earned a nickname that required zero explanation: The Glove. When Gary Payton decided to guard you, the ball was essentially already his. He just had not collected it yet.

Alongside him was Shawn Kemp, a power forward who dunked on people with a level of personal enthusiasm that suggested he genuinely enjoyed it every single time. And he did it every single game. Coach George Karl arrived in 1992, looked at what he had, and very wisely decided the best strategy was to let Payton talk and let Kemp dunk and then get out of the way. By 1996, the Sonics had sixty-four wins and were headed to the NBA Finals.

Their opponent was the Chicago Bulls, who had just finished a regular season so historically dominant that sports fans still argue about it at dinner tables today. Seventy-two wins. Michael Jordan in his prime. The basketball world had basically already ordered the Bulls their championship trophy and was debating where to ship it. Seattle looked at all of that and said: interesting, let us make this difficult for you. The Sonics pushed the Bulls to six games, with Payton locking up Jordan so effectively in the final games that even Jordan admitted Payton had made his life hard. Seattle lost the series. But they made the greatest team of that era earn every single point, and if you are going to lose, losing to the 72-win Bulls after pushing them to six games is a pretty respectable way to do it.

4. The Move That Broke a City

In 2006, a group of investors from Oklahoma City bought the Seattle SuperSonics for 350 million dollars, and Seattle fans felt uneasy from the exact moment the news broke. The new ownership group was led by Clay Bennett, an Oklahoma City businessman who had watched the New Orleans Hornets temporarily use his city as a home base during hurricane relief the previous year. Oklahoma had discovered it loved NBA basketball during that stretch. Bennett had taken extremely detailed mental notes.

What followed was one of the messiest relocations in sports history, and it was not subtle about being messy.

Negotiations over a new arena in Seattle fell apart loudly. The ownership made clear they were not especially attached to keeping the franchise in the Pacific Northwest. Seattle sued. Oklahoma City waited. After months of legal battles, a settlement landed in 2008: Oklahoma City would get the franchise, Seattle would receive 45 million dollars, and the SuperSonics name would legally stay in Seattle in case the NBA ever returned. Oklahoma City got the team. Seattle got the name and a check. Nobody in Seattle felt great about that math.

The final home game was exactly as emotional as you would expect from a city losing its only major professional sports franchise. Fans packed the arena knowing it was the last time. Kevin Durant, fresh off his rookie season and already looking like something from another planet, waved to the crowd as the buzzer sounded. The SuperSonics were finished. The building went quiet in that specific way that has nothing to do with the scoreboard. An entire basketball identity had just packed its bags and moved to Oklahoma. Seattle would not forget it. And honestly, you cannot blame them.

5. Thunder, Renegades, or Twisters

When the franchise touched down in Oklahoma City for the 2008-09 season, it needed everything from scratch. A name, colors, a logo, and most importantly a reason for a city that had never had its own NBA team to feel like this one was genuinely theirs. The team put together a list of sixty-four potential nicknames and opened the vote to fans. Renegades made the cut. Barons was in the mix. Twisters had genuine support, which would have been an excellent choice for a team playing in Tornado Alley, though perhaps slightly terrifying as a brand promise to visiting teams.

Thunder won by a comfortable margin, and honestly it is hard to argue with it. Oklahoma sits in a region where storms roll across the plains with real authority, where actual thunder is something locals know personally and take seriously. The state's 45th Infantry Division had long carried the Thunderbirds nickname, giving the name a local military connection that felt earned rather than invented. The new colors, navy blue punched up with a bold orange, looked sharp and completely distinct from anything Seattle had worn. The Thunder were not going to look like the Sonics in a new city. They were going to look like something entirely their own.

On the first day merchandise went on sale, the numbers broke records. Season tickets moved fast. When the Thunder played their first home game, the noise inside the building made it clear Oklahoma City had not just received a basketball team the way you receive a package you did not order. They had been waiting for this. They were ready. The SuperSonics were history. The Thunder were here. And a small city in the middle of the country was about to make the entire NBA take notice, whether the rest of the league was ready or not.

6. Kevin Durant: The Slim Reaper (2007-2016)

Kevin Durant is six feet ten inches tall and weighs around two hundred and forty pounds, which sounds impressive until you see him next to other NBA players and realize he looks like someone stretched a regular person on a medieval rack and handed them a basketball. He is impossibly long and impossibly thin, and opposing defenders spent years trying to figure out how a human being with that particular body shape could score from literally anywhere on the court. They never figured it out. He just kept scoring.

Durant was drafted second overall in 2007, first by Seattle and then, six days later, relocated along with the rest of the franchise to Oklahoma City. He was nineteen years old, already one of the most gifted scorers anyone had seen in years, and about to become the cornerstone of a franchise that was rebuilding from the ground up in a city that had never had an NBA team. No pressure. Durant averaged nearly twenty points per game in his first full season and then proceeded to improve every single year after that like he was following a carefully written schedule. He led the NBA in scoring four times in an Oklahoma City uniform. He won the league MVP award in 2014 with a speech that made half the arena cry, including several large professional athletes who would very much prefer you not mention it.

The Thunder built everything around Durant and the results were extraordinary right up until the moment he left in 2016 to join the Golden State Warriors, which is a story for Chapter 3. What matters here is what he built in Oklahoma City before he went. Durant gave a small market franchise its first genuine superstar, its first MVP, and its first trip to the NBA Finals. Oklahoma City will always be part of his story, whether he likes it or not.

Kevin Durant rises for a thunderous dunk. Long arms. Smooth power. When KD attacks the rim, defenders usually arrive a moment too late. Photo: Kevin Durant dunk. Photograph by Keith Allison. Licensed under CC BY-SA 2.0.

7. Russell Westbrook: Mr. Triple Double (2008-2019)

Russell Westbrook showed up to his introductory press conference as a Seattle SuperSonic in 2008, wearing a Sonics hat, and was told six days later that the team was actually moving to Oklahoma City. He took this information in stride and then spent the next eleven years playing every single basketball game like he had a personal grievance against everyone else on the court. This is not a criticism. It was genuinely thrilling to watch.

Westbrook is the kind of player who redefines what you think is physically possible. He was not the tallest player on the floor. He was not always the most technically polished. But he played with an intensity so concentrated it occasionally made referees nervous, and his athleticism was in a category that required its own zip code. He also became the most prolific triple-double machine in NBA history, averaging double digits in points, rebounds, and assists in three consecutive seasons from 2017 to 2019. The last person to average a triple double for an entire season was Oscar Robertson in 1962. Westbrook did it three years in a row. Oscar Robertson, a Hall of Famer widely considered one of the greatest players ever, reportedly watched this happen with his jaw on the floor.

He is also the franchise's all-time leading scorer, which feels important to mention because people sometimes forget it when talking about Durant. Westbrook logged 18,859 points in an Oklahoma City uniform, more than any player in Thunder history. He made eight All-Star teams, won the MVP in 2017, and played every possession of every game as if his entire personality depended on it. Which, honestly, it kind of did.

8. James Harden: The Beard Begins Here (2009-2012)

Here is a fun piece of trivia: one of the most prolific scorers in NBA history spent his first three professional seasons coming off the bench for the Oklahoma City Thunder, and during that time he was very, very good and almost completely taken for granted. James Harden arrived in OKC as a first-round draft pick in 2009 and immediately became the team's secret weapon, a reserve player who could change games in twelve minutes of action and then sit back down like he had not just personally disassembled the opposing defense.

The beard was already present and already remarkable. It has been one of the most famous features in sports for over a decade now, a beard so distinctive that it functions essentially as a logo. Small children recognize the beard before they learn his name. The beard has probably received fan mail.

Harden was so effective as a sixth man that he won the NBA's Sixth Man of the Year award in 2012, which sounds like a consolation prize until you realize how genuinely difficult that role is to execute at a championship level. He provided the Thunder with a luxury almost no team in the league had: a player talented enough to start anywhere else who was willing to embrace a supporting role and make the team dramatically better because of it. The Thunder made the NBA Finals in 2012 with Harden as their secret ingredient coming off the bench, and more on that particular chapter of Oklahoma City history shortly. That summer, OKC made the decision not to offer Harden the contract extension he was looking for, he was traded to Houston, and he immediately became one of the highest scoring players in the history of the sport. Oklahoma City has been thinking about that one ever since.

9. Shai Gilgeous-Alexander: SGA (2019-Present)

When the Oklahoma City Thunder traded Paul George to the Los Angeles Clippers in the summer of 2019, they received in return a player named Shai Gilgeous-Alexander, three first-round draft picks, two draft pick swaps, and two additional first-round picks via Miami. Most basketball analysts looked at this trade and said: well, at least they got some picks. The picks were nice. The player turned out to be slightly more important.

Shai Gilgeous-Alexander is from Hamilton, Ontario, which makes him Canadian, which makes the fact that he is a 2025 NBA MVP and a champion feel like a very large plot twist for a league that has historically been dominated by American players. He is long and fluid and plays with a pace so effortlessly controlled that scoring thirty points looks, from the outside, roughly as stressful as picking up a coffee order. He led the league in scoring during the 2024-25 season with an average of 32.7 points per game. He won the MVP award. He won the Western Conference Finals MVP. He won the NBA Finals MVP. He then signed a contract extension worth 285 million dollars, one of the highest annual salaries in NBA history, and Oklahoma City celebrated so loudly the whole state probably heard it.

He was also in the middle of a historic consecutive games scoring streak that had already passed Wilt Chamberlain's record by the time this book went to print, and more on that particular achievement in Chapter 3. For now, what matters is this: the Thunder gave up one star and got back the player who would bring them their first championship in Oklahoma City. Sam Presti, the general manager who made that trade, has never once said the words "you're welcome," but he is absolutely thinking them.

10. Jalen Williams: J-Dub (2022-Present)

Jalen Williams was drafted twelfth overall in 2022, and a significant portion of the basketball world immediately forgot about it. He had played college basketball at Santa Clara, which is a fine university but not exactly the program that produces players who end up being cornerstones of championship rosters. Scouts had questions. Analysts had concerns. Jalen Williams had absolutely no interest in any of that and went about proving everyone wrong with the quiet efficiency of someone who had been planning this for years.

He averaged 21.6 points, 5.3 rebounds, and 5.1 assists per game during the Thunder's 2024-25 championship season, making him one of only five players in the entire league that year to average twenty points, five rebounds, five assists, and one and a half steals simultaneously. The other four players on that list were Luka Doncic, SGA, James Harden, and Nikola Jokic. Jalen Williams was keeping company with the most elite offensive players in the sport, and a large percentage of casual fans still needed to Google his full name. He made his first NBA All-Star team that season, finally receiving the widespread recognition that Thunder fans had been shouting about for two years.

What makes Williams particularly valuable to Oklahoma City is everything he does that does not show up in the scoring column. He guards multiple positions. He makes smart decisions. He does not need the ball in his hands to affect the game. Alongside SGA, he gives the Thunder something most teams dream about having: two players who are each good enough to be the best player on most rosters, sharing a locker room and apparently getting along just fine. Championship teams are built on exactly that kind of luxury, and the Thunder have it in abundance.

11. Durant's MVP Season: The Year OKC Announced Itself

By the 2013-14 season, the rest of the NBA had been quietly hoping Kevin Durant was just very good rather than historically great. The 2013-14 season removed all doubt and did so without any subtlety whatsoever. Durant averaged 32 points per game, led the league in scoring for the fourth time, and played at a level that made defending him feel less like a basketball problem and more like a philosophical one. How do you guard someone who can score from anywhere, at any time, against anyone, while also being too long for normal human blocking attempts? The answer, it turned out, was that you mostly could not.

When Durant was named the league's Most Valuable Player that spring, he gave an acceptance speech that became one of the most talked-about moments in NBA award show history. He worked through his teammates one by one, thanking each of them personally and describing what they meant to him. Then he got to his mother, Wanda Durant, who had raised him largely on her own and sacrificed enormously to give him every possible opportunity. He looked at her and said: you are the real MVP. Half the arena cried. The other half was already crying and pretending they were not.

Oklahoma City was at its absolute peak. Durant was the best scorer in the world. Westbrook was playing like someone had installed a turbo engine where his regular engine used to be. The Thunder looked like a dynasty in the making. It was a genuinely wonderful time to be an OKC fan, which makes what happened next feel even more specifically unfair.

12. The 2012 NBA Finals: So Close, Yet So Far

Time travel back to the spring of 2012, and you would find an Oklahoma City Thunder team that had just done something remarkable. They had beaten the San Antonio Spurs in the Western Conference Finals, which in 2012 was the basketball equivalent of climbing a mountain that most people thought was unclimbable. The Spurs had Tim Duncan and Tony Parker and Gregg Popovich, who has spent the better part of three decades making opposing coaches look like they forgot to prepare. OKC beat them in six games and earned a trip to the NBA Finals in just their fourth season in Oklahoma City.

Their opponent was the Miami Heat, featuring LeBron James, Dwyane Wade, and Chris Bosh, a collection of talent so deliberately assembled that half the league was still furious about it. The Thunder won Game 1. Oklahoma City celebrated like the championship was already settled. LeBron had other thoughts.

Miami won the next four games in a row and took the title in five games. LeBron James was outstanding throughout, playing with the kind of focused determination that suggested he had spent the entire year reading scouting reports in his sleep. OKC was young, talented, and had just been schooled by a team that was simply a little further along in figuring out how to win the biggest games. The Thunder went home disappointed but not devastated. They had Durant and Westbrook and Harden, they were all still young, and the general feeling around the franchise was that this was not the last Finals trip. They were right about that. It just took a lot longer than anyone expected.

13. The Night Durant Left

In June 2016, the Oklahoma City Thunder held a 3-1 series lead over the Golden State Warriors in the Western Conference Finals. For those unfamiliar with basketball math, winning three games before your opponent wins four means you are one victory from the NBA Finals. The Thunder had three chances to close it out. They lost all three. It was the kind of collapse that makes sports fans stare at walls and question their life choices.

Then came the summer. Kevin Durant, the franchise cornerstone, the player OKC had built everything around for nine seasons, announced he was leaving as a free agent to join the Golden State Warriors. The same Golden State Warriors who had just beaten him. He was going to team up with Steph Curry and Klay Thompson and Draymond Green, forming a group so stacked with talent that the rest of the league immediately began doing the math and frowning. Oklahoma City fans were devastated in a way that was completely understandable, given that Durant had seemed like someone who would retire as a Thunder for life, and also given that he was leaving to join the specific team that had just eliminated them.

The reaction around the NBA was loud and largely unkind. Fans in Oklahoma City burned jerseys, which is the classic sports heartbreak response that never actually makes anyone feel better but continues to happen anyway. Durant went on to win two championships with Golden State. Oklahoma City went back to square one, held by a general manager named Sam Presti who looked at the rubble and started quietly making plans that would take years to pay off. Those plans, it turned out, were spectacular.

14. The Rebuild Nobody Saw Coming

After Durant left, the Oklahoma City Thunder did
something that surprised almost everyone who follows
the NBA: they did not panic. They had Russell
Westbrook, who responded to losing his best friend and
co-star by averaging a triple-double for an entire
season, which is the most Westbrook possible response
to adversity. They made the playoffs. They competed.
And behind the scenes, general manager Sam Presti
was assembling what would eventually become the
most quietly brilliant collection of draft assets in
modern NBA history.

When Paul George, who had arrived in OKC as a
legitimate star, was traded to the Los Angeles Clippers
in 2019, the return package included Shai
Gilgeous-Alexander and a set of draft picks so extensive
it looked like a ransom note. When Westbrook was
traded to Houston that same summer, more picks came
back. When Chris Paul moved through on his own way
somewhere, more picks arrived. Oklahoma City was
essentially running a draft pick factory, and while
analysts spent a year or two questioning the strategy,
Presti was quietly selecting players in the lottery who
turned out to be exactly as good as he thought they
were.

The Thunder finished with one of the worst records in the league in 2020-21, which was the plan. They needed high draft picks to build around SGA, and they got them. They selected Chet Holmgren, a seven-foot center who moves and shoots like someone programmed him in a laboratory specifically to create problems for opponents. They added Jalen Williams. They drafted Cason Wallace. Each piece clicked into place with the kind of methodical precision that made it clear Presti had known exactly what he was doing the whole time. He just needed everyone to wait long enough to see it.

15. Oklahoma City, We Are the Champions

The 2024-25 Oklahoma City Thunder won sixty-eight regular season games, the most in franchise history up to that point, and entered the playoffs having spent the entire season beating teams by an average of nearly thirteen points per game. Thirteen points. Per game. For the whole season. The rest of the NBA was essentially background music.

They rolled through the first three rounds of the playoffs with the kind of defensive intensity that made opposing offenses look like they were trying to solve a puzzle someone had switched the pieces on. Then came the NBA Finals against the Indiana Pacers, a team that had spent the entire playoffs making improbable comebacks and refusing to behave like they were supposed to lose. Game 1 went to Indiana on OKC's home floor. The series went to seven games. Oklahoma City, which had been picked to win the whole thing before it started, was suddenly in a proper fight.

Game 7 was played at Paycom Center on June 22, 2025, in front of a crowd that had been waiting seventeen years for this exact moment. Indiana's star point guard Tyrese Haliburton went down with an injury in the first quarter and did not return, which was genuinely difficult to watch, but the Pacers kept competing anyway because apparently that is just what they do. The game was tied deep into the third quarter before SGA hit a three-pointer that cracked the game open. Chet Holmgren finished with five blocked shots, a Finals Game 7 record. OKC closed it out 103-91. The Thunder were champions.

Chapter 4: Rumble, Rituals, and Oklahoma Thunder Culture

16. Rumble the Bison: The Most Electrifying Mascot in the Business

Every NBA team has a mascot. Most of them are fine. They wave flags, throw t-shirts into the crowd, and do a reasonable job of keeping things entertaining during timeouts. Rumble the Bison is not most mascots. Rumble has an origin story, an award, and a legend that was apparently passed down for centuries around Native American campfires, which is not a sentence you can say about Benny the Bull.

According to the official Thunder lore, Rumble traces back to a powerful storm that struck the Arbuckle Mountains of Oklahoma. A great bison herd was scattered by the chaos, and one lone bison stayed behind to help the others escape down a ravine. He got them out. Then, trapped alone at the top of the mountain with boulders blocking his path down, he climbed to the very peak and was struck directly by lightning. Most creatures do not survive that. Rumble gained superpowers. He can walk on two legs, perform acrobatic stunts from ninety-five feet above the arena floor, and play the drums. The lightning strike was clearly a very good investment.

Rumble debuted on February 17, 2009, descending from the arena rafters on a platform and immediately playing a drum solo on the court. He won NBA Mascot of the Year just six months later, which remains one of the fastest mascot career trajectories in recorded history. He has since won the Community Impact Award, appeared at over one hundred and ninety events in a single season, and interacted with roughly seventy-five thousand fans per year. Somewhere in the Arbuckle Mountains, the other bison are watching and wishing they had stayed behind too.

17. Stand Until They Score: Paycom Center's Greatest Tradition

Most NBA arenas are loud during big plays. Paycom Center is loud before the game even starts, which sets a tone immediately and lets visiting teams know they are in for a very particular kind of evening. But the tradition that defines the Thunder home experience above all others is simple, completely free, and requires exactly zero athletic ability from the participants.

Fans at Paycom Center stand and cheer from the opening tip until the Thunder score their first basket. The entire arena, on its feet, making noise, refusing to sit down until Oklahoma City puts points on the board. It sounds like a small thing. It is not a small thing. When seventeen thousand people are standing and screaming in a building specifically designed to amplify crowd noise, the decibel level becomes something visiting players describe afterward using words like overwhelming and honestly a little concerning. The tradition is borrowed directly from college basketball culture, which makes sense given that Oklahoma does not have a shortage of passionate college sports fans looking for somewhere to put all that energy.

The nickname Loud City was not invented by a marketing team in a conference room. It was earned, game by game, season by season, by a fanbase that shows up with a level of enthusiasm that has made seasoned sports journalists stop and write lengthy pieces about it. One famous account from the 2012 NBA Finals described fans arriving forty-five minutes early and clapping through the entire warmup. The writer predicted they would burn out before halftime. He was wrong. His eardrums were apparently never the same.

18. Oklahoma's Team: One City, One Team, Zero Chill

Here is a piece of context that explains almost everything about Thunder culture: the Oklahoma City Thunder is the only major professional sports franchise in the entire state of Oklahoma. No NFL team. No MLB team. No NHL team. Just the Thunder. This is not a footnote. This is the entire explanation for why OKC fans behave the way they do, and why the relationship between this franchise and this city is unlike anything else in professional basketball.

In most major American sports markets, the local NBA team competes for attention with football teams, baseball teams, hockey teams, and about forty other entertainment options. Thunder fans do not have that problem. When basketball season arrives in Oklahoma City, there is one team and one conversation, and the entire region locks in with an intensity that visiting analysts consistently describe as startling. The college football rivalry between Oklahoma and Oklahoma State divides the state right down the middle for most of the year. The Thunder unifies it. Republicans and Democrats in Oklahoma disagree on most things. They agree on the Thunder. That is genuinely remarkable and slightly more impressive than the championship.

Sam Presti, the general manager who built this team, requires every new Thunder player to visit the Oklahoma City National Memorial, which honors the victims of the 1995 bombing that devastated the city. The message is clear: before you play here, understand who you are playing for. It is the kind of thing that turns a basketball team into something larger than basketball, and it is a significant part of why Oklahoma City produces the most devoted fans in the league. They are not just cheering for wins. They are cheering for themselves.

19. The Name on the Door: Welcome to Paycom Center

Paycom Center has been the home of the Thunder since 2008, when the franchise arrived from Seattle and needed somewhere to play immediately. The arena was already there, originally opened in 2002 as the Ford Center, built without luxury boxes because Oklahoma City decided from the start that no fan should be too far from the action. That decision turned out to be an excellent one, both for atmosphere and for the extremely loud noise that results from packing seventeen thousand people into a space where the upper level is not actually that far from the court.

The building has gone through a few name changes over the years, moving from Ford Center to Oklahoma City Arena to Chesapeake Energy Arena before landing on Paycom Center in 2021. Paycom is a software company based right in Oklahoma City, which means the arena's naming rights belong to a local business rather than a national corporation, which is a small detail that Thunder fans tend to appreciate. The building is currently scheduled to serve the team until a brand new arena opens around 2028 to 2029, at which point Paycom will retire its naming rights and the new building will get a fresh identity. We'll get into that in Chapter 5. Whatever it ends up being called, Oklahoma City will pack it every single night.

20. Thunder Up: The Battle Cry That Became an Identity

Every sports team eventually develops a rallying cry. Most of them are variations on the same basic concept: say the team name loudly and add some enthusiasm. Thunder Up is not that. Thunder Up is two words that somehow manage to contain an entire identity, a feeling, a philosophy, and a mild threat all at the same time. When seventy thousand people chant it during a championship parade, it sounds like the city itself is speaking.

The phrase arrived naturally with the team and became embedded in Oklahoma City culture faster than almost anyone expected. It appears on signs, tattoos, business marquees, and the occasional church marquee, which says something about how seriously this city takes its basketball. Local restaurants put it on their menus. Politicians use it in speeches. Children learn it before they learn the state capital, which is also Oklahoma City, but that is beside the point.

What makes Thunder Up genuinely interesting is that it works equally well as a greeting, a declaration, a command, and a celebration. You can Thunder Up before a game, during a game, after a win, and apparently also at a road race, since Rumble the Bison has been known to show up at the Oklahoma City Memorial Marathon and Thunder Up at runners who are significantly less enthusiastic about it at mile twenty-two. It is a phrase that belongs entirely to one city and means something real to the people who live there. That is harder to build than a championship roster, and the Thunder managed to do both.

Chapter 5: The Reign Continues

21. SGA's Historic 2024-25 Season: The Year Everything Happened at Once

Some NBA seasons are good. Some are great. Shai Gilgeous-Alexander's 2024-25 season was the kind that requires its own Wikipedia category and a separate document just to list all the things that happened in it. He led the league in scoring with 32.7 points per game, won the regular season MVP award, won the Western Conference Finals MVP award, won the NBA Finals MVP award, and then finished it all off by signing a four-year contract extension worth 285 million dollars, the highest annual salary in NBA history at the time. He did all of this while being twenty-six years old and from Hamilton, Ontario. Canada is still processing it.

He became only the fourth player in NBA history to win the regular season MVP, the Finals MVP, and the scoring title in the same season. The other three are legends whose names get mentioned in conversations about the greatest players who ever lived. He also became just the second player since Michael Jordan to average at least thirty points per game on fifty percent shooting while adding five rebounds, five assists, one and a half steals, and one block per game. When the comparison list for your season is Michael Jordan, the season was not normal.

The championship parade through downtown Oklahoma City drew hundreds of thousands of people, and SGA waved a Canadian flag the entire time, which was both extremely on-brand and deeply appreciated by a country that had been waiting a very long time to see one of its own lift the trophy. Canada got Steve Nash's MVP awards. Canada got this. Canada is doing fine.

22. The 127-Game Streak: Longer Than Anyone in History

Wilt Chamberlain scored at least twenty points in one hundred and twenty-six consecutive games between 1961 and 1963, and for sixty-three years that record sat untouched. Various players took runs at it and fell short. The streak became one of those numbers that felt permanent, the kind of record that gets mentioned alongside DiMaggio's hitting streak and Wayne Gretzky's points totals as something that probably just lives there forever.

Shai Gilgeous-Alexander broke it on March 12, 2026, scoring at least twenty points for the one hundred and twenty-seventh consecutive game. The streak had started on November 1, 2024, and had run through an MVP season, a championship run, a contract extension, the start of a new season, and approximately sixty-three years of NBA history. During those one hundred and twenty-seven games, Oklahoma City went one hundred and two wins and twenty-four losses, which means SGA was not just scoring twenty points a game, he was doing it while his team was historically dominant. Wilt Chamberlain's Warriors went sixty-six and sixty during his streak. SGA's Thunder went one hundred and two and twenty-four. The basketball was also apparently better.

What makes the streak genuinely remarkable beyond the raw number is the consistency required to sustain it. Injuries happen. Bad nights happen. Games where everything goes wrong happen. Over one hundred and twenty-seven games across parts of two full seasons, none of those things stopped him from reaching twenty points. Wilt Chamberlain was a seven-foot one inch giant who dominated the sport physically in ways nobody has matched since. SGA is six foot six and gets to twenty points the way a chess player wins a match, by making the right moves at the right time until the problem is simply solved. Different eras, different methods, same record. Just kidding. New record.

23. The Young Core: Built to Last

One of the more entertaining things about the Oklahoma City Thunder's championship roster is how young it was. The Thunder are the second-youngest champions in NBA history, a distinction that sounds impressive until you realise it also means several of their key players were still figuring out how to drive at the start of the rebuild. Chet Holmgren, the seven-foot center who finished Game 7 of the Finals with five blocked shots, a Finals Game 7 record, was twenty-two. Jalen Williams was twenty-three. Cason Wallace, who had three steals in the first quarter of Game 7, was twenty-one.

Holmgren deserves particular attention because he is genuinely one of the strangest and most entertaining players in the modern NBA. He is seven feet tall and weighs around two hundred and twenty pounds, which means he has the wingspan of an aircraft but the build of someone who ate salad for four years straight. He moves like a guard, shoots like a wing, blocks shots like he has been personally offended by them, and plays with a confidence that suggests he has absolutely no interest in the traditional learning curve that most seven-footers go through. When he descends from the rafters at the new arena, the bison will have competition.

The depth of young talent surrounding SGA gives the Thunder something most championship teams lose immediately after winning: a reason to believe the next few years will be just as good as the last one. Oklahoma City did not trade away their future to win in 2025. They built from the ground up, developed everyone, kept everyone, and won anyway. Sam Presti has been right about everything for seventeen years. At some point it stops being luck.

24. A Brand New Home for a Championship City

Paycom Center has served the Thunder well since 2008, but Oklahoma City decided that a championship city deserves a championship arena, and in December 2023 the voters made that decision official. Nearly seventy-one percent of Oklahoma City residents voted to approve a one-cent sales tax to fund a new downtown arena. Not to maintain the existing one. To build an entirely new one. From scratch. By choice. Because that is the kind of city Oklahoma City has become.

The new arena, designed by MANICA Architecture and currently under construction downtown, will be thirty percent larger than Paycom Center at seven hundred and fifty thousand square feet. It features a three hundred and sixty degree glass curtain wall with panoramic views from every concourse, a grand entrance podium, and a design concept apparently inspired by Oklahoma sunsets, which is the kind of detail that makes architects very happy and basketball fans slightly confused but ultimately supportive. The Thunder ownership group contributed fifty million dollars toward the project, the first time in Oklahoma City history that a team owner has contributed to a publicly owned arena.

The new building is targeted to open around 2028 to 2029, at which point the Thunder have committed to staying in Oklahoma City for twenty-five years, potentially through 2053 and beyond. A city that in 2008 had never hosted an NBA team of its own now has a franchise committed to staying for at least another generation, a brand new arena going up downtown, and a championship banner already hanging in the rafters. Not bad for a place that once nearly ended up being called the Oklahoma City Twisters.

25. Back-to-Back Dreams

Winning one championship is hard. Winning two in a row is the kind of thing that gets entire documentary series made about it and earns teams a permanent spot in the argument about the greatest teams ever assembled. Only the 2016-17 and 2017-18 Golden State Warriors have done it in the modern era, and they had to acquire Kevin Durant, who Oklahoma City knows a thing or two about losing, in order to pull it off.

The 2025-26 Thunder entered their title defence having lost essentially nobody from their championship roster, which is not something most champions can say. SGA signed his extension. Jalen Williams was back. Chet

Holmgren was healthy. Alex Caruso, the veteran who had to explain to his teammates how to open champagne bottles after the 2025 title, was still there providing experience and apparently continuing his tutorial series. The team started the new season faster than any Thunder team in history and spent the early months being talked about in the same breath as the legendary Bulls and Warriors teams that had set the standard for sustained dominance.

Whether the Thunder win another championship or not is something time will answer more reliably than this book can. What is already certain is that Oklahoma City has become one of the most respected small-market franchises in the history of professional basketball. They rebuilt the right way, they won the right way, and they did it all in a city that simply refused to be overlooked. Thunder Up.

Bonus Trivia Quiz!

You think you are a true Thunder fan? Try this bonus quiz!

1. What was the Oklahoma City Thunder originally called before they moved from Seattle?

A) The Seattle Storm
B) The Seattle SuperSonics
C) The Seattle Thunderbirds
D) The Seattle Renegades

2. What year did the Seattle SuperSonics win their only NBA championship?

A) 1975
B) 1979
C) 1983
D) 1996

3. What industry inspired the name Seattle SuperSonics?

A) Shipbuilding
B) Logging
C) Aerospace and aviation
D) Coffee

4. Which legendary Seattle coach served as both a player and head coach at the same time?

A) George Karl

B) Bill Russell

C) Lenny Wilkens

D) Jack Sikma

5. How many potential nicknames did fans vote on before the Thunder name was chosen?

A) 12

B) 32

C) 64

D) 100

6. What was Gary Payton's famous nickname?

A) The Hammer

B) The Glove

C) Downtown Gary

D) The Wall

7. How many times did Kevin Durant lead the NBA in scoring while playing for Oklahoma City?

A) Two

B) Three

C) Four

D) Five

8. Russell Westbrook averaged a triple-double for how many consecutive seasons?

A) One
B) Two
C) Three
D) Four

9. Before being traded to Houston, what award did James Harden win with the Thunder?

A) Defensive Player of the Year
B) Most Improved Player
C) Sixth Man of the Year
D) Most Valuable Player

10. Which team did the Thunder lose to in the 2012 NBA Finals?

A) The San Antonio Spurs
B) The Boston Celtics
C) The Golden State Warriors
D) The Miami Heat

11. What is the name of the Thunder's official mascot?

A) Blaze the Buffalo
B) Rumble the Bison
C) Bolt the Bear
D) Storm the Stallion

12. According to official Thunder lore, how did Rumble the Bison gain his powers?

A) He was bitten by a radioactive basketball
B) He ate an entire bag of pre-workout
C) He was struck by lightning while saving his herd
D) He was trained by the 45th Infantry Division

13. What is the famous Paycom Center crowd tradition where fans stand and cheer until the Thunder score their first basket?

A) The Opening Roar
B) The First Bucket Stand
C) The Thunder Salute
D) The Loud City Rise

14. How many points per game did Shai Gilgeous-Alexander average during the 2024-25 season to lead the league in scoring?

A) 29.4
B) 30.8
C) 32.7
D) 34.1

15. How many consecutive games did Shai Gilgeous-Alexander score at least twenty points, breaking Wilt Chamberlain's record?

A) 112

B) 119

C) 124

D) 127

Super Fan Secret Challenge

Only a true Thunder fan will know this.

(No Answer Provided)

During the 2025 NBA Finals Game 7 victory celebration, the Thunder's champagne bottles caused a small problem in the locker room. Which veteran player, the only one on the roster who had previously won an NBA title, stepped in to show his teammates what to do?

A) Russell Westbrook

B) Alex Caruso

C) Luguentz Dort

D) Isaiah Hartenstein

Answer Key

1. B) The Seattle SuperSonics

2. B) 1979

3. C) Aerospace and aviation

4. C) Lenny Wilkens

5. C) 64

6. B) The Glove

7. C) Four

8. C) Three

9. C) Sixth Man of the Year

10. D) The Miami Heat

11. B) Rumble the Bison

12. C) He was struck by lightning while saving his herd

13. B) The First Bucket Stand

14. C) 32.7

15. D) 127

NBA PLAYOFF BRACKET

First Round	Semifinals	Conf. Finals	Finals	Conf. Finals	Semifinals	First Round

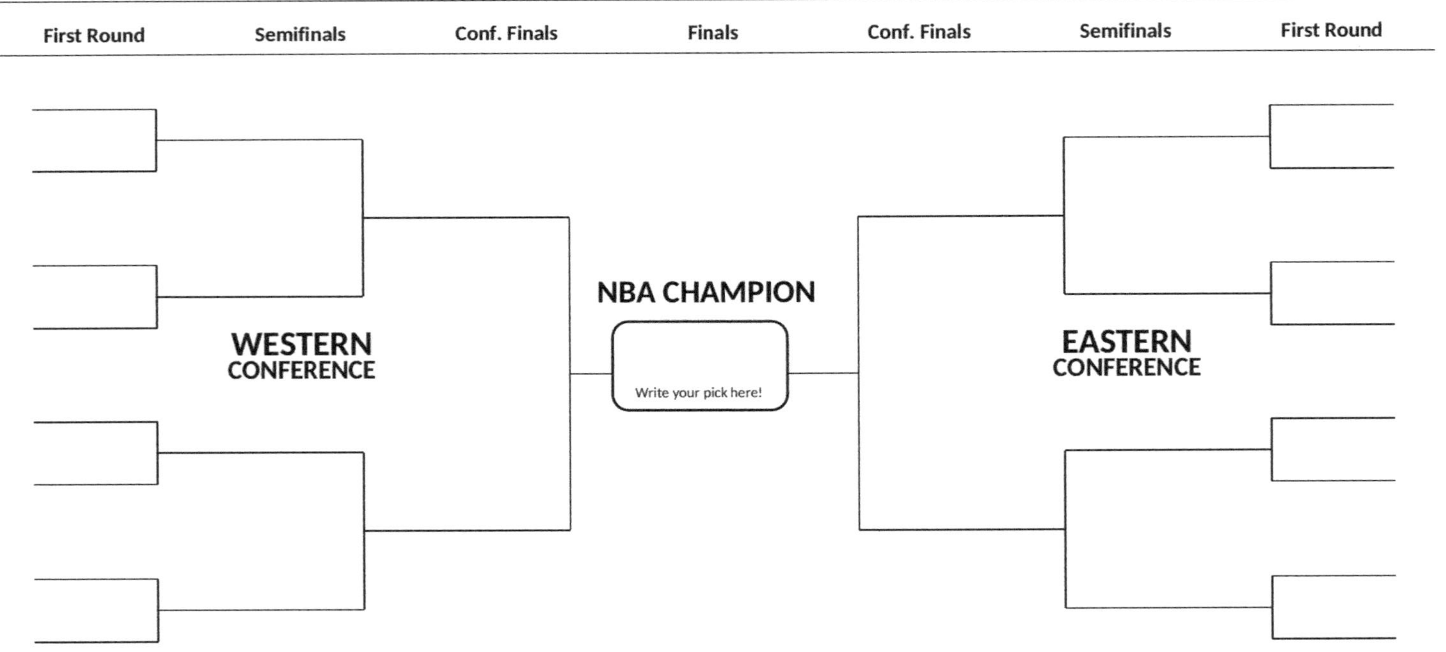

* Fill in your picks and try not to argue with your friends about it!

Part of the Fun Fan Facts: The Unofficial Sports Guide Series

Be the Boss of the Playoffs

You've broken down the matchups. You know which superstar takes over in the fourth quarter. You've seen the bench units that quietly decide series. You've watched the adjustments coaches make when their backs are against the wall.

Now it's time to stop watching and start deciding.

On this page, you are not just a fan. You are the Head Coach drawing up the last play with three seconds left on the clock. You are the GM who built this roster. You are the analyst who saw it all coming.

This is not just filling out a bracket.

This is building your championship run.

Sixteen teams enter the NBA Playoffs. The path is brutal. Best of seven. No shortcuts. No hiding. Every round gets louder, harder, and more personal.

This bracket is your Playoff Control Room.

The Game Plan

1. Survive Round One: Start with the opening round. Which matchup is going seven games? Who has the closer? Who folds under pressure? Make the calls.

2. Feel the Momentum: As you move into the Conference Semifinals and Conference Finals, things change. Role players become heroes. Stars feel the weight. Trust your reads.

3. Own the Finals: Trace your picks all the way to the NBA Finals. When the confetti falls and the trophy is raised, you'll find out who earned it.

House Rules: Circle your boldest upset. That is your official "I knew it" moment.

Choose Your Weapon: Pencil if you want flexibility. Pen if you trust your instincts. Sharpie if you believe in chaos.

Because once the playoffs tip off, there is no rewinding Game 7.

Make your picks. Trust your basketball brain. And let the playoff drama begin.

Fun Facts Wrap-Up

You made it through! You're officially a true superfan! Now it's time to put your knowledge to the test. Share these facts with friends and see who really knows their team best.

Love the series?

Your reviews help other fans discover Fun Fan Facts. If you enjoyed this book, we'd really appreciate you sharing your thoughts and leaving a review.

Want more Fun Fan Facts?

Scan the QR code below to visit our site and explore bonus trivia, challenges, and special extras - including new teams, future series, and collectible fun as they're released.

Collect All the Fun Fan Facts Series!

Check off every book you read. See the full set on Amazon. Search "Fun Fan Facts Jake Liam."

World Cup 2026 Edition

☐ Algeria
☐ Argentina
☐ Australia
☐ Austria
☐ Belgium
☐ Brazil
☐ Canada
☐ Cape Verde
☐ Colombia
☐ Croatia
☐ Curaçao
☐ Ecuador
☐ Egypt
☐ England

☐ France
☐ Germany
☐ Ghana
☐ Haiti
☐ Iran
☐ Ivory Coast
☐ Japan
☐ Jordan
☐ Mexico
☐ Morocco
☐ Netherlands
☐ New Zealand
☐ Norway
☐ Panama

☐ Paraguay
☐ Portugal
☐ Qatar
☐ Saudi Arabia
☐ Scotland
☐ Senegal
☐ South Africa
☐ South Korea
☐ Spain
☐ Switzerland
☐ Tunisia
☐ United States
☐ Uruguay
☐ Uzbekistan

World Cup 2026 Group Edition

☐ Group A
☐ Group B
☐ Group C
☐ Group D

☐ Group E
☐ Group F
☐ Group G
☐ Group H

☐ Group I
☐ Group J
☐ Group K
☐ Group L

English Football Edition

- ☐ Arsenal F.C.
- ☐ Aston Villa F.C.
- ☐ Chelsea F.C.
- ☐ Everton F.C.
- ☐ Fulham F.C.
- ☐ Liverpool F.C.
- ☐ Manchester City
- ☐ Manchester United
- ☐ Newcastle United F.C.
- ☐ Tottenham Hotspur
- ☐ West Ham United
- ☐ Wrexham A.F.C.

NBA Edition

- ☐ Atlanta Hawks
- ☐ Boston Celtics
- ☐ Brooklyn Nets
- ☐ Charlotte Hornets
- ☐ Chicago Bulls
- ☐ Cleveland Cavaliers
- ☐ Dallas Mavericks
- ☐ Denver Nuggets
- ☐ Detroit Pistons
- ☐ Golden State Warriors
- ☐ Houston Rockets
- ☐ Indiana Pacers
- ☐ LA Clippers
- ☐ Los Angeles Lakers
- ☐ Memphis Grizzlies
- ☐ Miami Heat
- ☐ Milwaukee Bucks
- ☐ Minnesota Timberwolves
- ☐ New Orleans Pelicans
- ☐ New York Knicks
- ☐ Oklahoma City Thunder
- ☐ Orlando Magic
- ☐ Philadelphia 76ers
- ☐ Phoenix Suns
- ☐ Portland Trail Blazers
- ☐ Sacramento Kings
- ☐ San Antonio Spurs
- ☐ Toronto Raptors
- ☐ Utah Jazz
- ☐ Washington Wizards

About the Author

Jake is a 13-year-old sports fan who loves football, American football, and basketball. He plays soccer as a goalie and dreams of one day playing for West Ham United and helping teach kids to love the game. His passion for sports runs in the family - his dad was a professional baseball player, and his stepdad sparked his love for West Ham. Through the Fun Fan Facts series, he shares the fun and excitement of sports with fans everywhere.